Edward B. Hunt

Union Foundations

A study of American nationality as a fact of science

Edward B. Hunt

Union Foundations
A study of American nationality as a fact of science

ISBN/EAN: 9783337034153

Printed in Europe, USA, Canada, Australia, Japan

Cover: Foto ©Suzi / pixelio.de

More available books at **www.hansebooks.com**

UNION FOUNDATIONS:

A STUDY

OF

AMERICAN NATIONALITY

AS

A FACT OF SCIENCE.

BY

CAPT. E. B. HUNT,
CORPS OF ENGINEERS, UNITED STATES ARMY.

NEW YORK:
D. VAN NOSTRAND, 192 BROADWAY.
LONDON: TRÜBNER & CO.
1863.

ELECTROTYPED BY
SMITH & McDOUGAL,
82 & 84 Beckman-st,

NOTE.

As the following discussion of the scientific bases on which our nationality has rested and must rest, was written in September, 1862, the partial coincidence of certain views herein set forth with those embodied in a portion of the President's Message of December, 1862, must be regarded as a natural agreement, and as an evidence that these views are truthful and necessary results of candid study.

The Editor's Table of Harper's Magazine, for February, 1863, contains a condensed re-casting, by an able hand, of many facts and views presented in this study, and I can but hope that the popular audience thus reached, as well as the readers of the following pages, may find therein, not only food for reflection, but new courage, and new hope, amid the gloom and distraction of a trying hour.   E. B. H.

NEW HAVEN, CONN., *Jan.* 20, 1863.

ABSTRACT OF CONTENTS.

"I am compelled to ascribe the frame of this system to an intelligent Agent."—NEWTON. *Second Letter to Dr. Bentley*.

"For it became Him who created them to set them in order."—NEWTON. *Optics, 31st Query*.

"If the laws of Nature, on the one hand, are invincible opponents; on the other, they are irresistible auxiliaries."

"There is something in the contemplation of general laws, which powerfully induces and persuades us to merge individual feeling, and to commit ourselves unreservedly to their disposal; while the observation of the calm, energetic regularity of Nature, the immense scale of her operations, and the certainty with which her ends are attained, tends, irresistibly, to tranquilize and reassure the mind, and render it less accessible to repining, selfish, and turbulent emotions."—SIR J. F. W. HERSCHELL, *on the Study of Natural Philosophy*.

"Science may attempt to comprehend the purposes of God, as to the destinies of nations, by examining with care the theatre, seemingly arranged by Him, for the realization of the new social order, toward which humanity is tending with hope. For the order of Nature is a foreshadowing of that which is to be."—GUYOT'S *Earth and Man*.

UNION FOUNDATIONS.

TRUTH is King: Cotton and Corn are subjects. Nations, like individuals, owe their first allegiance to truth, wisdom, and duty. Now, while our nationality is being tested and proved, while trials beset, and great convulsions perplex us, let us, with all-enduring faith, hold fast to the eternal principles of reality and right. More than ever amid the varying phases of a fluctuating contest, do we need to stand fast on eternal foundations. Calmly trusting that God will not permit chaos to conquer His own divine order, we must defend those social and political principles which we have sincerely and gratefully accepted as our national heritage and trust. As helpful to this end, we now propose to examine in the cold light of Science, those grand Natural realities which, through the ages, must constitute our *Union Foundations*.

Science interprets God. He has wrought into the fabric of material nature those ideas and designs which He has chosen to adopt. The inorganic and organic worlds are thus records of Divine thought and intent. Science reads these records. Through long historic ages the mind of man has been accumulating knowledge and slowly gathering to itself the means for deeper and clearer insight. Science stands in the attitude of devout inquiry, within the courts of the grand temple of Nature, attentive to every whisper of the Divine oracle. Her profoundest faith is in God, who, through special arrangements of material masses, and infinitely diversified mechanisms of organic structure, has expressed His own mind, will, and nature. Through patient toil and earnest interrogation, Science has learned much. The work of Nature-interpretation goes on with increasing success and with ever-expanding faith in the Designing Author. Intelligent communion with Him augments and grows intimate. Loftier views and grander insights throng upon us. The higher scientific mind of to-day has learned to see in and through "the invariable order of occurrence" which prevails in Nature, a grand expression of God's supreme will, unfolding itself by a secular progress. What once was Fate is now our Father's will. There is no more brute matter; we see only materials through which the Divine will expresses itself in language which, however imperfectly comprehended now, will, in the unfolding order of ages, tell forth that Wisdom which was able to incorporate all progress in a germ.

Man is part of Nature, and human history is the culmination of Natural history. Divine designing has wrought out in man its completest earthly expression. A long-drawn geologic progress and a parallel organic progress have reached their climax, and perhaps their limit, in the human period. Man, from his Eden origin to his expanded and complex present, has half consciously lived out into an epic record the Divine legation impressed upon, expressed through, and vitalized in human nature. Through myriad years of preparation, the earth had been prophetically forming for man's habitation, and now, for six thousand years, he has been expanding over its surface, and through all fluctuations has been shaping it to his needs. God introduced man upon earth when it had become fitted to be his habitation. We but express the profound and fundamental conviction of that noble school of Physical Geography whereof Humboldt, Ritter, and Guyot may be named as expositors, when we say that the earth was not only deliberately framed and organized to be man's habitation, but so specially combined as to prescribe and prophesy the actual order of human history. Man and his earth-home were framed in the same mutual adaptation and coordination which we are wont to see between the house and its inhabiting family. When, therefore, we study the relations between a nation and the country it inhabits, we are, in strict science, striving to read the Divine will as concerning that nation. Earnest piety, duty and profound policy concur in demanding that nations shall conform to the Divine will as expressed in their conditions of habitation. The nation which, with true insight, sees and accepts the Divine purpose in its existence, can not fail of that best prosperity possible for it, which our Father had, from the measureless past, held in store for its benediction. On the other hand, a nation which blindly combats its God-given conditions of existence, can not fail to suffer frustration and those bitter punishments, masked, perhaps, under the guise of seeming prosperity, which are kindly ready to constrain transgressing communities back into the right path of national life.

A survey of human history shows a well-defined and easily-comprehended progress, from the rude beginnings among nomadic tribes, to the present state of high, but unequal, civilization. America had only a provisional or transient population of Indians, until Columbus, three hundred and seventy years ago, initiated a European knowledge of our continent. Amid the growth and decline of Old-World nations, the knowledge of a New World was held in reserve, until the time should come for its colonization under conditions conformed to the Divine plan of development. It was not until its actual discovery that the intellectual, social and political progress of Western Europe had formed a civilization fit to be transplanted into our reserved continent. Not until man had attained worthy ideas of liberty and order; not until political culture had ripened into a systematic blending of individual freedom with organized government, was it Divinely permitted, that the permanent population of this continent should be introduced. Then, by degrees, the pressure of over-population combined with the love of enlarged liberty to afford the emigration needed for the introduction of a vigorous colonization. Our whole history has plainly shown our national function to be one which concerns humanity at large. Starting with a clear field and with the benefit of all Asiatic and European experience, it was the mission of America to carry forward social organization beyond any Old-World type. The Spanish-American States, having failed to achieve such progress, the execution of this continental mission has devolved wholly on the United States. By our past history, we have accepted this mission, and, until 1860, we were apparently in the full tide of success. It is a distinctive feature of the true American that, under his daily activities, he cherishes a deep, abiding consciousness of, and faith in, this grand relation of his country to the whole human progress. This is to him not only a grand and hopeful, but a fearfully responsible destiny. Americans can not, if they would, hide from themselves the fact, that the future of a continent is divinely intrusted to their fidelity, and that humanity at large has a special claim on them truthfully to serve its cause.

The scientific study of nature throws much light on the question as to "what constitutes a State." Minds which have grown familiar with the organic kingdom and the grand principles of organic growth and structure, can hardly fail to recognize that nations are social and political organisms, and that the entire human family constitutes an organism of still higher generality. Germs and eggs are developed by growth into mature, prolific organisms. So do nations, from germinal beginnings or colonies, develop, by vital growths, into imperial organizations, which, in turn, establish colonies, and finally die by violence, disease or senility. The Sothic period was, by the ancients even, called the lifetime of great nations, as illustrated in the Persian, Grecian and Roman empires. Our nation has passed through its feeble infancy, its colonial boyhood, its bold launch into independence, and its early years of young manhood. Nations, like other organisms, pass from a primal simplicity of structure to an increasing complexity of parts and functions. Nations too, like organisms, at first manifest but slight mutual dependence of parts, but with their growth into complexity, their functions and subdivisions develop an increasing inter-dependence, until the total life at last rests on the functional perfection of each portion. Man's practical vocation is to labor. As society progresses, labor is subdivided or specialized, and the economic prosperity of a nation depends on the perfection of this labor-specialization, or on the proper correlation of its specialties. So too in plants and animals, does progress in the specialization of functions and functional organs and in their normal correlation, increasingly mark every step from germination to maturity.

In all animal embryos, a *serous* layer and a *mucous* layer are formed around the yolk. The mucous membrane develops into the nutritive system, and evolves all the organs for preparing food. The serous membrane develops the nervous, muscular, and osseous systems, all directing their actions outward. So too, in a nation of high organization, there is a food-producing class, and there is a class supplied with food, whose labors of manufacture, skill and administration give back to the food-producers needful compensations. In the further embryonic progress, the *vascular* layer appears between the serous and mucous layers, and develops into the system of blood vessels, whose function is to take up the food supplied through the mucous or nutritive system, and to carry or circulate it to the serous or nervo-muscular system, or wherever it is needed for growth or repairs. Thus in the social growth, commerce

arises to interchange food and materials, whether raw or manufactured. As growth progresses, the nutritive, nervo-muscular, and circulating organs grow more complex and specialized, just as in a mature community, agriculture, manufactures
and commerce grow ever more multifarious and special in their
matter and methods. The sap of plants and the blood of animals are the analogues of the mass of products **circulated by**
commerce. Liebig compares the blood discs, which, without
"an immediate share in the nutritive process, are the medium
for all the sustaining activities of the blood," to money, which
is "the medium of all activity in the life of the state." The
channels of blood circulation grow complex, as organization approaches the higher and maturer types; so, in an advanced society, do the highways of commerce grow intricate. The *main*
channels of commercial circulation are capacious, direct, crowded, and rushing. *Main* arteries, like railroads, send rythmic
pulses. From main arteries to the capillaries, from railroads
to the footpaths, there is increasing ramification, curvature,
contraction, slowness, and irregularity.

The most important analogy between a national and an
animal organism is that existing between the governmental
structure and the nervous system. Nervous organisms, in all
animals, consist of *ganglionic centres* and *nerve trunks*, the
ganglions being cellular and the nerves fibrous. The afferent
or sensory nerves bear in impressions to the nervous centres,
and the efferent or motor nerves bear outward from the same
centres excitations to movement by muscular contractions. In
many animals these ganglionic centres are repeated freely
without diversity of function, and in other species these multi-
plied, homogeneous ganglions are continuously connected by
nerve trunks. As we rise from the simpler to the more complex and highly organized animal types, the multiplication of
ganglionic centres is more and more designed to control special

functions by special ganglions. Thus, as we approach the higher forms, not only do we find special ganglions for deglutition, respiration, and locomotion, but ganglions of special sense, as sight, hearing, taste, &c. Just in proportion as animal structures rise toward higher types, do some of the anterior ganglions develop into preponderance; passing from an inappreciable superiority in the lower forms, up to the fully developed brain of man. Structural rank can be almost measured by brain-preponderance. As multiplication of ganglions without specialization of function marks low or rudimentary organization, so do minute ganglionic specialization and unification through brain-government indicate high organic rank and effective endowment.

In a nation, the governing centralizations are the ganglions; the representative agencies which inform and prompt to action are the afferent nerves, and the executive agencies which enforce law are the efferent nerves. A single absolute head, a patriarch or barbaric king, forms a one-ganglion government. A multitude of heads essentially independent, a league of barons bound only by some outside pressure, is analogous to animals having many ganglions of like function, such as the inferior *articulata*. When one baron among many grows to superior strength and influence, he becomes the cephalic ganglion, head or king. When his dynasty is established and its strength fully acknowledged, the brain-predominance becomes fixed and a high, articulate structure appears. As the subordinate repositories of political power take special state functions, the vertebrate structure appears. When deliberate legislation on wise, constitutional foundations supervenes, the function of the cerebrum is typified, and pure mind frames the measures which dominant will energizes as effective law.

It is important to remark that, in an extended country like ours, the geographical subdivisions do not conform to diversities of political functions. Throughout the country, states have severally identical functions, as have the counties in a state, and the towns in a county. The organic interpretation of our republican government may be thus stated. Convenience dictates subdivision of areas **into states, counties and towns. The town** is a pure democracy, and the people act in mass. **The coun-** ties act in such functions as towns cannot, and counties can, appropriately exercise. The states act in such functions **as** counties cannot, and states can, fitly fulfill. **The general** government acts in such functions as the states cannot, and the general government can, effectively discharge. The principle is that of graduation of governing functions by locality, so that each grade shall exercise those, and only those, which are appropriate to it. To centralize *all* government for a vast area, in a single absolute head, is utterly subversive of freedom, and is only possible by absorbing into the nervo-motor system of the centralized head so much of the nation's life and strength as will crush out its diffused vitality. Governmental diffusion by ganglionic graduation to the greatest convenient extent, gives to all the largest freedom, and im-**poses** on each-grade of governing centres only such a minimum and adapted charge as belongs to its place in **the scale.** To the individual is thus left all the freedom **possible.** Organically speaking, this graduation of governing ganglions specializes their functions. Thus the individual, town, coun-**ty, state and** general government severally exercise the special functions appropriate to their places on **the scale. The** elective and representative process is functionally analogous to afferent nerve-action, by sending in to **the several** grades of ganglionic centres representative impressions from the people, as data for deliberative consideration. To this afferent system belong the various associations which embody the voices of the manifold special interests blended in a community, outside of its technical political structure. The brain-functions, of intelligent deliberation upon representative impressions and of volition in legislation, being performed, executive agents act the motor-nervous part in the practical execution of law. In the normal exercise of specially assigned functions, each grade of ganglions commands those below it, and obeys those above it on the scale.

It is to be noted that each of these political ganglions is cerebral. Cerebration is only centralized so far as concerns the centralized functions. *Special cerebration in graduation* seems to be the organic definition of our form of government. We have before indicated functional specialty and cerebral predominance as the criteria of dignity in organic types. The signal blending of both in our government, by the introduction of systematic *sub-cerebration* and of *graduated governing functions*, is organically a great advance over previous systems. Should complexity be objected to it, we need but remark that increase of structural complication is an invariable attendant on organic elevation. Our system certainly rests on the presumption of a general loyalty in each component to its assigned part; just as, in all high organisms, each organ must do its work, or all will suffer. It is a truly significant fact, that this system of graduated government should have taken shape at the precise time it did, and in the country which emphatically, by its vast future, seemed to demand it.

The views now imperfectly stated are not barren. Nothing can make the heresy of secession seem more heretical than to test its application in our government, when viewed as an organism. Were we but a polype nation, fissiparous division would not be unnatural. Were we but some brainless, articulate organism, we might be cut in two and each half might become a living whole. That sub-cerebral states should assume superiority over the cerebral general government, is not less monstrous than the fantasy of a peaceful, painless dismembering of a high political organism. Treason seemed almost to have found an anesthetic which would enable a nation of high and sensitive structure to be cleft in twain, unconscious of the dividing edge.

Secession theories rest on the postulate of a nation *manufactured* at a certain date. *Nations grow: they are not made.* True organisms, they, like all animate beings, grow from embryo to old age. Their governments are *vital* realities; not parchments nor bargains. Our Constitution as framed and signed was the written statement, the formal expression of the goverment organically embodied in our people. The framers, with wonderful sagacity, drew forth the logic of facts as they stood, and shaped our governing agencies in exquisite adaptation to the growing and future nation. To all this obligation of fitness was superadded that of plighted faith, of solemn compact. But the Constitution is no mere contract between huckstering states, to be broken on shallow pretexts of interest or caprice. Above every sanction of consent, it expressed the grand governing system, which was then and is now a natural fact in our people. Under this formula, we have grown into an expanded national development, and are now bound in a living unity, which admits of severance only on the same surgical conditions which attend all organic amputations. We shall do well ever to bear in mind this living, organic nature of our government, and not to rest an unreasoning faith on the mere *verba scripta* of the Constitution. This instrument, with wondrous insight, provides for its own modification, to insure its permanent agreement with the natural, organic constitution of our people in all stages of our growth. Too exclusive an attention to the historic phases of our political organism, and too lawyer-like a concentration on the written charter which formalized it,

have perhaps blinded our statesmen to the profounder organic
entity, which lives in our people, and which, as it then ex-
isted, was so happily appreciated by the framers. To exalt
legal formalism above *vital realism* is to frustrate Nature,
or to breed liberating revolutions.

Definiteness of external form and external protecting envel-
opes, are among the most distinguishing and universal traits
of individual organisms. From seed-time to sapless age,
every plant not only has the defined form of its species
throughout its entire development, but it exists under the
protective covering of a skin, shell, or bark. The tender
germ is enfolded in the secure heart of the seed, and the vital
circulation of the growing bark is covered by a hard, protecting rind, which serves only for defense. The egg, whence
all animal life emanates, is encased in a shell or protective
layer, under cover of which the embryo develops an outer
defensive skin, while all the most vital and vulnerable mem-
bers are formed in the central cavity. From the embryonic
ovisac to the wrinkled skin of old age, the same protective
policy is consistently exhibited throughout the entire animal
kingdom. The skins and shells of radiates, the shells of mol-
luscs, the rings of articulates, the skins, hair, and feathers of
vertebrates, concur in testifying that organic life is only possible for individuals possessing properly defined outer boundaries, and externally guarded by adequate protective envel-
opes against the manifold dangers that surround them.

So is it with a nation. National life is conditioned on definite exterior boundaries, and on adequate protective fron-
tiers. Organic analogy indicates that nations should only
vary their boundaries in conformity with the conditions of ex-
pansion by healthful growth. A policy of ambitious conquest,
an ungoverned greed of territory, find no sanction in organic
law. That a growing nation should expand into such needed

2

other, demanding a national dismemberment and an independent sovereignty for the seceded states. Even were we indifferent to the dignity and integrity of our government, and ready by a total sacrifice of our self-respect to seek peace on any terms, we could hardly concede the division called for. Any attempt to trace a boundary would raise insuperable difficulties. Delaware, Maryland, Kentucky and Missouri, which have never enacted the secession juggle, would be vehemently claimed as due to the South. We should be expected, either to abandon our capital, or to leave it under the guns of a foreign power. Fortress Monroe and the Norfolk Navy-yard would be required at our hands. Western Virginia, including the Baltimore and Ohio railroad, would be graciously accepted. A joint interest in the navigation of the Ohio might be kindly conceded us, but when we reach the Father of Waters, we must at once consent to intersect it by a foreign boundary. West of the Mississippi, there would appear to be no clue to a boundary except to yield whatever might be asked. In the Gulf we should be invited to relinquish Pensacola, Tortugas and Key West. The time would hardly have come to make a *mare clausum* of the Gulf, but the great North-West would most truly have become a *terra clausa*. The Pacific States, having lost all faith in, and respect for, the remains of the United States, would of course set up for themselves.

When secession was inaugurated, the cotton states were to cut loose and the border states were to keep the peace and protect Cottondom by interposing a neutral ground. When the epidemic took hold of the border states, slavery itself was to fix the boundary. The north line of the slave states was then the definite cleavage-trace accepted by the South, when a more vaulting ambition did not purpose to annex and provincialize the upper valley of the Mississippi. This simple plan has failed. Four slave states have not seceded, one has split and one is in large part reclaimed. The loyal states have fought valiantly for the pristine Union, and the Upper valley of the Mississippi is fully purposed to tolerate no foreign domination of its great river. There is no indication that even a simple, geometrical line of true political separation could be drawn; and even were such a trace agreed upon, it could not possess, in even the most moderate degree, the proper requisites for a defensive frontier. It is a physical fact that there is no such separating line across the territory of the United States; no possible frontier on which the parts of a divided union could rest in mutual security. Had we then every disposition to concede nationality to the seceded states, we could find no line which would serve us as a defensive boundary. We should open ourselves to attack not only from the South, but from the South reënforced by such European allies as might join flags with slavery. Perhaps combined British and Southern attack on three sides might endanger our dismembered nationality. We think it could not; but we are sure that we should show a signal lack of wisdom were we now to make such an attack possible.

Nor could any supposable separating line be permanent. Nature has given no hint of any such deliberate purpose. The elements of the present contest are not of a character to rest side by side in peace, out of respect to some wire-drawn parallel of latitude of treaty adoption. History repeatedly shows, how in far less " irrepressible conflicts," strong physical boundaries have failed to arrest border raids, and chronic recurrences of hostility. We could never bring ourselves to regard any separating line as for ever obligatory. There can be no boundary between the United and seceded States, which will rise above the rank of a *belligerent compromise line*; and no possible peace, *through disunion*, can be more than a *truce*.

This is a solemn and irrefragable fact; a fact, consequent not on feeling only, but on imperious natural realities, which must inspire and govern our national future. In order to a clearer appreciation of this momentous declaration, we will briefly consider some leading general features **of American** Physical Geography and Social Development.

We will first state some prime data and principles **of Physical** Geography. The land masses of the Earth compose six single or three double continents: Asia-Australia, Europe-Africa, and North and South America, whose respective **areas** in geographical miles, as given by Guyot are, Asia, 14,128,-000; Australia, 2,208,000; Europe, 2,688,000; Africa, 8,720,000; North America, 5,472,000, and South America, 5,136,000. Humboldt deduced the following average elevations above the sea: Asia, 1,151 feet; Europe, 671; North America, 748, and South America, 1,132. Their respective lengths of shore-line and areas in geographical square miles to each mile of shore-line are, Asia, 30,800 and **459**; Australia, 7,600 and 290; Europe, 17,200 and **156**; Africa, 14,000 and 623; North America, 24,000 and 228, and **South America**, 13,600 and 376. The general course **of the** Old World mountain-ranges is latitudinal; the **great Andes** and Rocky Mountain backbone of the New World, **is nearly** meridional. The three northern continents are temperate and arctic; **the three southern are** tropical and sub-tropical. The historic course of empire is westward, along the north **temperate zone.** Cold closes the great arctic plains to **human** habitation; heat gives the torrid zone chiefly to the tropical **races.** Civilization has lingered near shores through Southern Asia, the Mediterranean basin, Western Europe, and North America. Sea-coasts, islands, peninsulas, and river valleys, have attracted and governed man's migrations, and developed his faculties. The freely intersected and vastly diversified surface of the Old World along the historic zone, has stimulated man's physical and mental powers, thus originating and ripening his civilization.

The general structure of the North American Continent is strikingly simple. The Sierra Madre and Rocky Mountain system, extending 4,000 miles north-westerly from the Isthmus to the Arctic Ocean, is the grand axis of upheaval. A vast triangular plain, resting on this great mountain barrier, as a base, projects its vertex outward to the remote coast of Labrador. This magnificent *continental plain*, having an average elevation above the sea, of between 600 and 700 feet, and nowhere in mass exceeding 2,500 feet, unlike the vast, bleak, sterile and frozen table-lands of Asia, which in Thibet reach an elevation of 14,000 feet, has every orographical, climatic, and fertile requisite for playing a master part in the grand drama of human progress. The table-lands of Bavaria and Spain are elevated much above even the summit lines of this great American expanse. Except in a few limited mountain ridges, this area nowhere loses its productive capacity by reason of its altitude; nor do we, on the other hand, find disproportionate spaces sacrificed to swamps.

The general distribution of this continental plain is in two great slopes, declining respectively toward the Gulf of Mexico, and toward Hudson's Bay, and the Arctic Ocean. A low east and west swell, without any well-defined ridge or crest, traverses this plain. Starting from the high base of the Rocky Mountains, between the parallel head-waters of the Missouri and Sasketachewan Rivers, where it is about 3,000 feet high, this swell divides the Missouri head-waters from those of the Red River of the North, sinking near the latter to 1,350 feet, and rising around the head-waters of the Mississippi to about 1,700 feet. A short distance west of Lake Superior, this swell divides near the source of the Mississippi,

elevated 1,680 feet, and forks around the basin of the great
Lakes and the St. Lawrence.   The south ridge divides the
Lake and Ohio tributaries at an elevation of from 1,000 to
1,300 feet, the Genesee and Alleghany Rivers at 1,488 feet,
sinks in the Hudson and Champlain Valley to 140 feet, and
rises opposite Quebec to 1,500 feet.   The north fork of this
swell, dividing the Lake and Lawrentian basin from the Hudson's Bay basin, sinks near Lake Simcoe to 1,100 and 1,200
feet, and rises again opposite Quebec to 1,500 feet. As we
proceed from the treeless polar plains of the Mackenzie River
basin, southerly to the Gulf of Mexico, we traverse 2,400
miles of our great continental plain, nowhere rising above
an elevation of 1,700 feet, nowhere observing any bold con-
trasts or transitions, and yet, by the whole transit, we pass
from arctic mosses to tropic palms.   The east and west profiles of this plain exhibit a slight general declivity eastward,
from the Rocky Mountains to the Atlantic. They also show
a great variety of features which, however, leaves almost the
entire area within fertile conditions. It would seem that
Providence designed throughout this continental plain, to de-
rive meridional variety from simple climatic gradations, and
latitudinal variety from diversity of surface features.

The North American continent consists of the following
subdivisions.

The *Atlantic Slope*, passing from the St. Lawrence down
the coast, including Florida and a portion of the Gulf slope
to Mobile Bay, is drained by rivers with short courses, running in general perpendicular to the coast. This inclined
slope or plain, varies from 50 to 200 miles in width, and the
elevation of its upper margin ranges from 140 to over 1,000
feet. It is throughout its whole extent, free from well marked
transverse ridges, and profiles parallel to the coast will
show a plain-like continuity, intersected by no effective

separating features. The ocean frontage constitutes an effective union bond, by connecting this narrow slope in a coastwise navigation. This slope is like the half of a river basin; the coasting trade thus becomes analogous to the Mississippi river trade, and, like that, it is a powerful, natural connecting bond.

The *Appalachian Mountain System** extends in a N. E. and S. W. direction 1,300 miles, from the promontory of Gaspé on the Gulf of the St. Lawrence, to North Alabama where it sinks down into the approximately level strata forming the Gulf Slope. This mountain system consists of numerous nearly parallel ridges or folds, which are distributed into two general ranges, separated from each other by a narrow valley, nearly continuous from N. to S. and called the Appalachian Valley. This is locally known as the Champlain, Hudson, Kittatiny or Cumberland Valleys, the Great Virginia Valley and the Valley of East Tennessee, and it varies from an average breadth of 15 miles in the N. E. to about 10 in Virginia, and 60 in Tennessee. The chain of mountains to the eastward of this long valley, is made up of the Green Mountains in Vermont, the Highlands in New York, the South Mountains in Pennsylvania and the Blue Ridge in Virginia, North Carolina and Tennessee, including therein the Black, Iron, Smoky and Unaka Mountains. The White Mountains of New Hampshire, though partially isolated, belong to this chain, as being the central mass of a curved sweep in the Green Mountains and heights of land extending towards Gaspé. The chain of mountains west of the Appalachian Valley includes the Adirondack, Cattskill, Alleghany and Cumberland ranges, and extends, with some interruption, from Northern New York to Middle Tennessee. The Appala-

* See Prof. Guyot's admirable paper in the American Journal of Science, March, 1861.

chian Mountain system is remarkable as possessing no grand central ridge, but in its place appears the long valley or "negative axis" already described. A great number of parallel ridges, broken at short intervals, give a series of fruitful valleys and transverse gaps, through which river courses, highways and railroads find passage. The general tendency of the system is to greater elevation in going South, and the culminating region is at the southern end, where the great upheaval dies out abruptly into the Atlantic and Gulf plain. Black Dome, or Mitchell's Peak, the highest point not only of the Appalachian system but east of the Rocky Mountains, rises to 6,707 feet and at least twenty-four summits of the southern culminating section overtop Mount Washington, the culminating point of the northern section, which is only 6,228 feet high. Mount Mansfield, (the Chin,) the highest summit of the Green Mountains, is 4,430 feet high, and Mount Marcy, the apex of the Adirondacks, is 5,379. The western slope of the Appalachian Mountain system rises from, or dies into, a broad plateau base, averaging about 1,000 feet in elevation.

The portion of the great continental plain included between the Appalachian and Rocky Mountain chains, is composed of three great areas, forming the Hudson's Bay and Arctic basins, the Lake and St. Lawrence basin and the Mississippi basin.

The *Hudson's Bay Basin* offers so little useful land that, in a general view, it must be held as Arctic and nearly uninhabitable. More to the west, the *Arctic Slope* extends so much farther south, that the valley of the Red River of the North may have an important future.

The valley of the *Great Lakes and St. Lawrence* is unique in the world. The area of the lakes and river is 94,000 geographical square miles, (each equal to $\frac{436}{368}$ statute square miles,) while the entire basin of which they are part only measures 297,600 geographical square miles. That so small a surface should feed such large reservoirs, seems remarkable even when we regard them as simple river expansions. The area of this basin equals 10 Po basins, 4½ Rhine, 7 Elbe, 1½ Dnieper, and 37 Connecticut basins. Considering the small evaporation in this latitude, it is not perhaps mysterious that one-third the total area of this basin consists of water evaporating surface, besides which the Niagara and St. Lawrence are duly supplied. Lake Ontario is 231 feet high and 6,300 geographical square miles in area; Erie, 565 and 9,600; St. Clair, 570 and 360; Huron, 600 and 20,400; Michigan, 600 and 22,400; Superior, 630 and 32,000. The drainage summits along the rim of this basin being only 1,500 feet or less in elevation, all fertile lands therein offer a promise of tillage, after yielding their present wealth of forest products. This wealth, intercepted from the sea in great part by the rapids and ice of the Niagara and St. Lawrence, has found a signal natural compensation in that remarkable depression of the Appalachians which made the Erie and Oswego Canal outlets possible.

The *Mississippi Basin** includes most of the vast plain between the Appalachian and Rocky Mountain systems. Its area is 1,244,000 statute square miles and exceeds that of the whole continent of Europe, exclusive of Russia, Norway and Sweden. The Amazon basin alone upon earth exceeds it, and this has more than once and a half its development. The frozen Obi lacks some 70,000 square miles of equaling it, the La Plata is nearly ⅘, the Yenesei about ⅞, the Lena, Amour, Hoang-Ho, Yang-tse-Kiang and Nile, about ⅔ each, the Ganges less than ½, the Indus less than ⅓, the St. Lawrence and Lake basin less than ⅓, the Oronoco, a little over ¼,

---

* See the elaborate and important report of Captain A. A. Humphreys and Lieut. H. L. Abbott on the Mississippi River, 1861.

the Euphrates $\frac{1}{3}$, the Columbia and Rio Grande, each less than $\frac{1}{3}$, the Delaware, $\frac{1}{115}$, and the Connecticut $\frac{1}{120}$. On this vast space fifteen Rhine basins would find room, England and Wales might be twenty-one times repeated, and Continental France be six times superposed. Over 300,000 square miles* in Texas and New Mexico, belonging to the same structural category as the Mississippi Basin proper, are not included in these statements, and need not be separately discussed.

Ideas formed on the contracted scale of the river basins of Western Europe, need to be rudely shocked by forcible exhibits of the immense magnitudes of the Mississippi River system. Nor are conceptions based on the vast but sterile Siberian basins more adequate. The high plateaus and immense mountain spaces of Southern Asia, make even the rivers of China and India somewhat fallacious guides when we would investigate the capacities of the Mississippi basin for human habitation. There is no great river basin on the globe, which approaches it in its proportion of useful fertility, and especially in cereal productive power. In Illinois, for instance, corn can be raised at from eight to twelve cents per bushel and wheat at from twenty-five to thirty cents. Hardly an acre in the 55,405 square miles of this state is naturally unproductive; hence we need hardly wonder that in the last decade (1850–60,) her population has advanced from 851,470 to 1,711,753.

Throughout the Mississippi basin there is sufficient rain to give effect to the fertility of the soil. The annual average is 30.4 inches, of which one-fourth or 21,300,000,000,000 cubic feet are discharged into the Gulf. The annual rain-fall ranges from 68.4 inches in Louisiana to 13.1 at Fort Union. In the Ohio and Upper Mississippi Valleys, the annual fall ranges from 24.0 inches at Fort Snelling to 50.9 at West

* Statute miles are meant unless otherwise stated.

Salem in Southern Illinois. The decrease of rain-fall is progressive and general from South to North, and a prevailing decrease is observable in receding from the Mississippi River, either east or west, but it is far more marked as in going westward, we approach the Rocky Mountains. It seems to be a correct general statement of facts, that, starting from the mouth of the Mississippi, there is a gradual decrease of rainfall as we ascend the river or any of its tributaries.

It is not easy to realize the immense areas of the *secondary basins*, drained by the chief tributaries of the Mississippi. Starting at the mouth, we first reach the *Red River* basin, which contains 97,000 square miles, on which the average rain-fall is 39 inches, of which $\frac{1}{3}$ is discharged. The Red River is 1,200 miles long, and has its source 2,450 feet high though at Preston, 380 miles below, it is but 641 feet. The *Yazoo* basin has an area of 13,850 square miles, and an average rain-fall of 46.3 inches of which $\frac{2}{10}$ are discharged. At Horn Lake, 500 miles from its mouth, the Yazoo is 210 feet high. The *Arkansas* and *White River* basin has an area of 189,000 square miles, and an annual rain-fall of 39 inches, $\frac{1}{3}$ of which is discharged. The Arkansas has its source 1,514 miles from its mouth, and at the height of 10,000 feet. At Fort Atkinson, 1,095 miles from its mouth, it is 2,331 feet high, and its mouth is 162 feet high. The *St. Francis* basin measures 10,500 square miles, and has 41.1 inches annual rain-fall, $\frac{2}{10}$ of which is discharged. Its source is 380 miles from its mouth, is 1,150 feet, and its mouth is 200 feet high. The *Ohio* basin has an area of 214,000 square miles, and 41.5 inches of rain-fall, of which $\frac{8}{24}$ are discharged. The Ohio at Coudersport, 1,265 miles from its mouth, is 1,649 feet high, and its mouth, near Cairo, is 275 feet. At Pittsburg, 975 miles up, the elevation is 699 feet, and at Cincinnati, 515 miles up, it is 432 feet. The *Missouri* basin has an area of 518,000 square miles and an average rain-fall of 20.9 inches, of which $\frac{8}{20}$ are discharged. The Missouri is 2,908 miles long to its Madison Fork source, which is about 6,800 feet high, while Fort Benton, 2,644 miles up, is 2,845 feet, and the mouth near St. Louis, is 381 feet high. The *Upper Mississippi* basin, above the junction with the Missouri, contains 169,000 square miles, and has 35.2 inches rain-fall, of which $\frac{8}{25}$ are discharged. The river course is 1,330 miles, and its source is in a tributary of Itasca Lake, at the elevation of 1,680 feet. It rises in a region of lakes and swamps, entirely free from mountains. From source to mouth, the Mississippi River is 2,616 miles long, and the *Mississippi-Missouri River* is 4,194 miles long. The total length of all the streams in the Mississippi river-system could hardly be estimated, but it has been computed that they afford 40,000 miles of navigable water. Between the several tributaries of the Mississippi, the chief of which rise in the Appalachian and Rocky Mountains, there are no separating mountain ranges. The Ozark Mountains alone rise from this great basin, a short, limited and isolated range, without general significance. The Lake and Lawrentian Valley is as it were a counter-sloped tributary, and no emphatic separation distinguishes it, as may be realized when we remember that Bellefontaine, the highest land in Ohio, is only 1,400 feet high. Careful consideration of the several heights stated, will sufficiently indicate the general plain-like structure of the great area west of the Appalachians from which the river valleys have been excavated.

Nearly midway between the Mississippi River and the Pacific coast, the plain-like character which distinguishes the valley proper, disappears, abruptly in some parts, in others by degrees. This ill-defined line marks the base of the true eastern slope of the *Rocky Mountains*. We are still quite unable, confidently to generalize the features of the broad domain between that line and the Pacific, which is so complex in structure, and so imperfectly explored, that geologists must expend patient years of observation before attaining a reliable basis for idealization. Geographically, this region contains, within our boundaries, 980,000 square miles, and measures on its longest cross-section, from San Francisco via Salt Lake to Fort Laramie, about 1,000 miles, or 1,125 by extending it to the secondary range of the Black Hills. Its axis or general structural direction is north 20° west. This is but a section or fragment of the great mountain-system of the earth, represented on our double continent by the Andes, Cordilleras, and Rocky Mountains, and which as Lt. Warren remarks, is nearly on a great circle from Cape Horn north to Bherings Straits, and thence across Asia to Sumatra, thus ranging through two-thirds of the circumference of the globe. There has been so much theorizing without facts, and mapping without surveys, on this western portion of the United States, that limitation to realities is not now easy. The various Coast Survey, Boundary, Topographical and Pacific Rail Road surveys, afford much and almost the only reliable information in this field. With Lt. Warren's map and the Pacific Rail Road profiles spread before us, it still remains difficult securely to go beyond some crude discussion.

It will not be doubted that the mass between the western margin of our continental plain and the Pacific Ocean, belongs to a single vast upheaval, in which the entire cosmic, great-circle, mountain system participated. The knowledge actually obtained will, perhaps, justify us in tracing a structural analogy between the Appalachian and the West-American mountain system. We have defined the Appalachian system as composed of two parallel grand ranges, separated throughout by the Appalachian valley, all trending parallel

to the Atlantic coast. Similarly, we find running parallel to the Pacific coast, two grand ranges separated by a
broad elevated valley. The Cascade range, Sierra Nevada, Coast range, and the Peninsular range of Lower California, form a grand chain which, starting in the Arctic zone
and reaching its culmination in Mount St. Elias, thence
slopes downward and disappears under the sea in Lower California. The grand interior chain, consisting of the Rocky
Mountains, and Sierra Madre or Cordilleras, extends from
the Arctic Ocean to the Isthmus, rising gradually from the
north to its culmination in Popocatepetl, and thence declining to the moderate elevations at Panama. Both of these
chains are complicated and irregular in structure, and are
freely intersected by passes, and even by water-courses. Intervening between them is the broad, elevated, and irregular
valley of upheaval, drained in part by Frazers, Columbia,
and Colorado Rivers. It is possible that this valley may be
a true plateau, but the progress of exploration tends to take
from it this character, by interpolating subordinate intervening mountain-ridges, such as the Humboldt, Wahsatch, Blue,
Mogolton, and numerous other minor ranges already made
known. On each of the Pacific Rail Road routes explored,
four or more summits were crossed, and it can hardly be
doubted that the ultimate result of complete surveys will be
to define a great number of limited ridges intervening between the two grand chains, and observing a general law of
parallelism with them, complicated by some centres of upheaval from which mountain crests radiate. The analogy of
Appalachian structure may re-appear in a wave-system of
ranges and valleys, with transverse passes and over-lappings.

It may be remarked that there is a general elevation of this
grand valley from north to south. The great Columbia Plain,
west of the Spokane, on the Stevens' railroad route, is raised

at the highest 2,340 feet, and averages about 2,100. The upper valley of Snake River is about 2,500 feet; Salt Lake is 4,238, and Humboldt River Valley, also forming part of the Great Basin, averages about 4,300 feet. The valley of Grand River is about 4,500 feet, and the Colorado-Chiquito Valley, about 5,000. The plateau of the Sierra Madre, and the Llano Estacado or Staked Plain, are about 4,500 feet, while the Guadaloupe Pass, which connects these areas across the Eastern Mountain chain, is only 5,717. The table-land of Anahuac or Mexico, is from 6,000 to 8,000 feet high; the city of Mexico being 7,471. These average levels of the broadest known areas, which are here named in regular order, from north to south, indicate a general ascent southward through the West-American Valley; the apparent exception in the Sierra Madre plateau, being possibly a secular result of local diluvial waste. This upward slope tends to counter-act the increase of heat with diminishing latitudes, thus pre-serving a temperate climate even in Mexico.

An unfortunate result of the position and structure of the West-American Mountain and Valley system, is that a lack of rain and consequent sterility exists to some extent over all this region except along the narrow Pacific slope. It is too early to speak positively, but there is apparently little hope that a proportionate population can find support in this 900,000 square miles. Between the Rocky Mountain ridge and the western edge of the continental plain, is a sterile belt varying from 200 to 400 miles wide, in which poverty of soil and lack of rain conspire to prohibit extended culture. The same sad fate broods over a large portion of the Grand Valley, which has a sterile soil, and is cut off from rains by the moun-tains running North and South on each side. Winds from the Atlantic, almost discharged of moisture in their long transit over the Mississippi Valley, reach the mountain region with but little water for precipitation.   On the other hand, winds from the Pacific, being intercepted by the Cascade range and the Sierra Nevada, while they give rain to the Pacific slope, fail to transport and precipitate moisture in the amount needed for the great valley.   Enough is precipitated by the action ot the mountain crests to give fertility and especially grazing capacity to a limited area of valley slopes and bottoms, where the soil favors.   This amounts to a valuable natural provision for the mining population, which is sure to be required in developing a mountain mineral wealth now almost unknown; but cereals can never be largely produced in this region. The favored valley around San Francisco Bay, thanks to the moderate relief of the coast range, has a happy dispensation from sterility.   This basin and the Pacific slope or coast belt, averaging about sixty miles wide, within our boundaries, form the chief land of agricultural promise throughout this great western domain.   Enough is known to foreshadow a future of mining, with auxiliary agriculture and grazing, for the West-American mountain and valley system;   a future which will bond itself naturally and indissolubly to the fertile Mississippi Valley by the operation of the already initiated Pacific railroad.

Having reviewed the main physical or structural features of this continent, and especially of our own national domain, we are now entitled emphatically to renew the declaration that nature has provided no east and west line of separation between the seceded and loyal states. All the grand structural subdivisions of our territory, except the Lake basin, are essentially meridional in direction.   The Atlantic coast and slope, and the Appalachian Mountain system, run N. E. and S. W.   This mountain system has its southern extremity turned by the broad gulf slope, and it is so freely traversed by practicable routes, that even were it revolved into an east and west direction, it would be but an imperfect frontier. The great Mississippi basin has the axis or trunk of its tree-like river system, almost perfectly meridional. The Rocky Mountains, the great Western Valley, the Pacific mountain chain, the Pacific slope, and the Pacific coast, have a generally concurrent N. W. and S. E. direction. This *average meridional distribution* not only prevents any natural boundaries from east to west, but creates a singularly powerful system of bonds between the North and South zones of our domain. It would seem that the cosmic Designer shaped all the physical features of our country, as if purposely to stabilitate American unity against the disruptive tendencies of diversity in climate, interest, origin, or feeling.

The Atlantic coast navigation, penetrating on various lines far into the interior of the Atlantic slope, binds the portions of this long and narrow tract by an all-absorbing coasting trade. The railroad system east of the Appalachians strongly corroborates this sea-coast bonding, both by its routes parallel to the coast and by those which bring down their tribute from the interior to the coast as to a vast river. The Appalachian Valley converts even the mountain system which it divides, into a north and south bond, by the railroad route it offers.

It is impossible to over-estimate the influence of the Mississippi river-system in binding all the area drained by it, into a compact and powerful organic whole. The immense commerce already developed on the forty thousand miles of navigable rivers in this system, is but the twilight before the dawn. Every year of pacific union must expand its vast proportions, until the Gulf, the Florida Channel, and the Gulf Stream shall be known but as its crowded entrance way or outer mouth. Besides this exterior current of commerce, there is an interior interchange of such magnitude that the

analogy of the rain-fall, only one-fourth of which finds its way
to the Gulf, may perhaps, represent the relations of total and
exterior movement. The eye can scarcely inspect a map of
the Mississippi and its tributaries, without being struck with
its arborescent form. This tree-likeness, itself the analogue
of the system of blood vessels in animals, has a profound
meaning. It asserts to the eye, what experience has for years
been unfolding in fact, that this river system, this mechanism
for commercial circulation, is an organic unity, owing its
very vitality to that unrestrained freedom for self-develop-
ment, which it has hitherto enjoyed. To dismember it is
death ; to restrict it, is strangulation. To permit the mouth
of the Mississippi to be in foreign hands is to permit a grasp-
ing hand on our throat. That hand might not actually press
our jugular vein, but the indignity remains, and the threat
of strangulation is hardly less objectionable than the reality.
The men of the Upper Mississippi Valley can only look upon
a foreign custody of the mouth of their river system as an
outrage to be resisted forever. They instinctively and pro-
foundly feel that when God made the Mississippi, He also
made the Union, and that to sever what He so conjoined, is
to war against heaven, and to war as vainly as did Lucifer.
Divide the Mississippi ! better divide a tree at half its height
and expect the top to grow ! The ostentatious concession of
free navigation is like the politeness of a burglar, in asking
you to sup with him upon your own dainties and at your own
table.

As if to make more clear the indivisibility of the Mississippi basin, the actual railroad routes included, strikingly
resolve themselves into north and south lines, bonding the
Gulf and the Lakes in significant union. The organic and
indestructible unity of the Mississippi Valley would, by its
inherent vitality, be ever asserting itself against any lines of

separation our weakness or dereliction might inaugurate. He can have but slender comprehension of our physical geography, who does not recognize this unity, and who does not see therein a Divine assertion of the substantial unity of this continent. Just because the vast and fertile Mississippi basin is strictly a unit, must our country and the continent have a united future. This valley so largely exceeds the Atlantic and Pacific slopes, and the West-American valley, in productive resources, that its influence must be permanently dominant. This fact involves nothing alarming, as the bonds of union and amity, which have joined the eastern slope with the Mississippi Valley, and which, through the Pacific railroad, will increasingly bind the West-American system to it, are based in Nature, and are thoroughly reciprocal. The Rocky Mountains, indeed, furnish a perfect natural boundary, (the only one on our continent,) were separation thereon desirable, but even this divellent possibility will yield to the superior bonding force of that great destined highway, which, like an artificial river, will spread its branches along the Rocky Mountains, in the great western valley, and over California, Oregon, and Washington, developing their vast mineral resources, and returning food from St. Louis and manufactures from the east.

The east is bound to the Mississippi Valley by many other ties than lineage or consanguinity. Continuity is a powerful bond. From Boston to St. Louis, the traveler is conscious of no break. There are great diversities, but no place affords suggestions of boundaries, and, indeed, the bare idea of seeking a boundary between east and west, is physically even more absurd than the like search as between north and south. Stronger even than consanguinity, contiguity or constitution, is the bonding force of that vast system of travel and transportation between the Atlantic and the West, which

though now but partially developed, stands unrivaled in the
world. The Great Lakes were a partial answer beforehand
to the need of inter-communication between the East and West,
and will eternally enforce, as by Divine sanction, their friendly
and compact union. Niagara Falls, the rapids of the St. Lawrence, that river's ice-bound mouth, and the wondrous stretch-
ing forth of the Hudson valley toward Lakes Ontario and
Erie, form the God-given charter of New York city, and forever ordain it as the true outlet of the Great Lakes, and the
port of entry for our continent. It is the great American
metropolitan heart, through which the life-renewing streams
of domestic and foreign commerce must ever circulate in pul-
sating rhythm, along arterial and venous highways to and
from every portion of our vast continental plain. This can
best be appreciated as a fact by considering the magnitude
and growth of the lake trade.

The five lake States, in 1850, produced 252,000,000 bushels of cereals, and in 1860 the amount rose to 354,000,000.
The cereals carried on the lakes in 1861, amounted to
101,819,596 bushels, of which Chicago shipped 54,167,007,
Milwaukie, 18,778,629, Toledo, 18,706,510, Detroit,
7,167,450, and other ports, estimated, 3,000,000. In the eastward march of this commerce, Buffalo trans-shipped over one
half of the total by the Erie Canal, Oswego nearly one sixth
by the Oswego Canal, Dunkirk and Suspension Bridge one
eleventh by railroad, other points nearly one twelfth, and
one twelfth went down the St. Lawrence by Montreal. The
annual value of merchandise and agricultural products carried
on the lakes, is now between two and three hundred millions
of dollars. In 1861 the Erie Canal carried to tide-water
2,980,144 tons, of which 2,158,425 tons consisted of bread-
stuffs. The New York Central Railroad in 1861, delivered
435,956 tons of through down freight. The New York

Canal receipts have gone up from $1,723,945 in 1859 to $4,725,707 in 1862, to August. The toll receipts were $722,829 in the single month of July, 1862. Our exports of breadstuffs and provisions, almost entirely transported over the Erie Canal and the parallel railroads, was valued at $12,341,901 in 1821; $10,624,130 in 1836; $9,636,650 in 1838; $16,743,421 in 1845; $68,701,921 in 1847; $77,187,301 in 1856; $93,969,682 in 1861, and for 1862, a still larger aggregate will be reached. The cereal imports of Great Britain amounted to 37,918,000 bushels in 1846, when the corn-laws were repealed, and had risen to 115,059,000 bushels in 1860, the increase being largely derived from our inexhaustible stores. Russia, the great grain shipping country of the Old World, exported only 27,000,000 bushels in 1854, and 49,000,000 in 1857, or less than one-half our grain-crop moved on the lakes in 1861. Already the State of New York produces barely one third of the wheat it consumes, and New England only enough for three weeks' consumption. The total cereal products of the United States were, in bushels—

	1850.	1860.
Wheat	100,485,944	171,183,381
Rye	14,188,813	20,976,286
Indian Corn	592,071,104	830,451,707
Total	706,745,861	1,022,611,874

The value of flour and meal produced during the years ending July 1, 1850 and 1860, is thus distributed—

	1850.	1860.	Per cent. increase.
New England States	$6,320,486	$11,155,445	76.5
Middle States	68,483,179	79,086,411	15.5
Western States	42,673,992	96,038,794	125.0
Southern States	16,531,817	30,767,457	85.5
Pacific States	1,888,332	6,096,262	222.8
Total	$135,897,806	$223,141,369	64.2

The great fact stands out boldly that the West is not only to feed the East, but is to supply European, and especially British deficiencies. The wheat grown in Illinois, at twenty-five to thirty cents, and the corn for eight to twelve cents, by the mere movement of transportation, commands **New York** and European prices, **four or five** times the cost of production. Such being the vast importance and bonding **power of the** lakes, canals, and railroads, they become a perpetual **guarantee** of firm union between East and West. The Grand **Trunk** Railroad, the St. Lawrence and the Welland Canal, the Erie and Oswego Canals, the New York Central and Great **Western** Railroads, the New York and Erie Railroad, the Pennsylvania Central Railroad, the Baltimore and Ohio Railroad, with their several connections and extensions, constitute a system of east and west routes for travel or traffic, such as nowhere else exists; a system bonding **east and west, with a** force even exceeding the north and south bonding **force of** the Mississippi, and the parallel railroads. If any one thinks the great, dominating, prolific West will consent to be shut in by a foreign **South** and a foreign East, **he** is so blind that **he should be dumb.**

Western railroads are everywhere cheaply **constructed,** and Western rivers are gentle in slope and **therefore easy of** navigation, simply because the Mississippi **Valley is a great** plain; **thus throughout this area, free** inter-communication by locomotive and steamboat, is naturally provided. This same **plain-like** structure **also** forbids the general **prevalence of** water-power adapted to manufacturing uses. **But water-**power and coal are the only bases of large **manufacturing** organizations. Water-power being in **general** forbidden to the West by the same structure which **gives it fertility and** **free** inter-communication, it must **look** to coal for supplying the deficiency. **It has an enormous** area of coal strata, but it is a notable fact that the coal-beds grow less rich as we go west. Our country has 192,000 square miles of coal fields, which is twenty times the total European coal area. The Appalachian fields, extending from Pennsylvania to Tuscaloosa, contain 70,000 square miles, and in the Schuylkill anthracite basin, there are about fifty seams, twenty-five being workable. The Pittsburg bituminous field has twenty beds, ten being workable. The Michigan field of 15,000 square miles is poor, with only two or three workable beds. The Illinois, Indiana, and Kentucky basin, containing 50,000 square miles, has twelve beds, seven being supposed workable. The Western basin in Iowa, Missouri, and Arkansas, containing 57,000 square miles, has six or seven beds, three or four being supposed workable. We might thus infer that coal mining would be permanently most profitable toward the east, a view which is strikingly supported by the actual statistics of our coal production. The total coal product in 1850 was valued at $7,173,750, and in 1860, at $19,395,765. Of this last amount, Pennsylvania alone gave 75.9 per cent., consisting of 9,307,332 tons of anthracite, worth $11,869,574, and 66,994,295 bushels of bituminous, worth $2,833,859, or a total of $14,703,433. Virginia produced 9,542,627 bushels, worth $690,188, and Ohio 28,339,900 bushels, worth $1,539,713. These facts indicate that the Appalachian field is the great dynamic storehouse of our country, as it is the one best provided with transportation outlets by water.

The Appalachian Mountain system also affords most of the useful water-power within the United States, and its structure, especially in the Northern section, is remarkably adapted to produce convenient, constant, and sufficient water-privileges. When this combination of available water-power and productive coal strata in the eastern section of our country is considered, it is as manifestly the Divine plan that this should be the American manufacturing region, as it is that the prairies are designed for agriculture, the Gulf slope for cotton fields, or the West-American mountain regions for mining. New England and the Middle states are already conscious of their destiny. It is well known that England owes much of her present development to a happy conjunction of iron and coal beds, and to the ease of transportation given by her railway system and insular character. Pennsylvania, our iron and coal state, is in nowise less favored by nature. New England and New York, dowered with vast water-power and easy water and railway transport, lack nothing but time and a wise economy to complete the triumph in manufacturing production, already so well begun. If happily labor is dearer here than in Europe, wheat, cotton, and the American market are nearer. Political economy* demands that agricultural and manufacturing production should be brought into close neighborhood, and we cannot much longer sin against reason and nature by interposing two Atlantic voyages between the farmer and the factory, whenever this can be avoided. When God placed the Mississippi Valley alongside the Appalachian Mountain system, it was that raw material, manufactures, and food might sustain each other in friendly Union, while supplying man's chief wants by a free interchange within a single, happy nationality.

Among the most sacred duties of those who are specially charged with directing the future of our continent, is that of excluding the European system of great standing armies and armaments. If the "balance of power" system exacts such costly offerings, we cannot too energetically suppress all tendencies toward such a policy on American soil. Europe now maintains in its peace-armies, about four millions of soldiers,

* See Carey's Works.

and expends on its military peace establishments, exclusive of navies, about four hundred and sixty millions of dollars annually, besides the loss by time taken from industrial pursuits, which is estimated at one hundred and forty millions. Thus Europe is six hundred millions of dollars poorer every year because of its military organizations, besides the vast interest payments for old wars, and current naval expenditures. Each modification of the equilibrium between states results in wars more or less general and destructive. It were better for us, even on economic grounds, to fight out our present battle to the bitter desolating end, than to perpetuate war and armaments by now consenting to that division of domain which must bring upon us the European system of military establishments, debts, and wars. Our loss by the systematic abstraction of labor from production would in a few years exceed the cost of our present painful contest. Heaven help us if we are driven to exchange our old peace organizations for the exhaustive and demoralizing system which has long cursed European states, which now burdens them to the verge of bankruptcy, and which taxes labor to the last point of endurance in behalf of a squad of bondholders. The practical effect of preserving the Union intact, will be to save us from this fate, and to realize, so far as America is concerned, the project of a congress of nations, in behalf of peace, our general government being in fact our continental umpire.

The capacity of the United States to sustain population, is but imperfectly comprehended, even by our most sagacious minds. Looking exclusively to the capacity of our land for producing cereals, vegetables, and dairy products, the following distribution of our 3,306,865 square miles into four grades is a reasonable approximation. The first grade is entirely and hopelessly sterile, and may be assumed as including 306,865 square miles. The second grade, which we will assume at one million square miles, has but very slight productive capacity, but can raise grass, food, and forest products sufficient to support fifty persons to the square mile. The third grade, including probably a million of square miles, contains the inferior arable lands, which are, on an average, fully capable of supporting 150 persons to the mile. The fourth grade, including the remaining million square miles, consists of the rich arable lands, capable of sustaining at least 400 persons to the mile by existing modes of culture. This estimate will give a total population within the United States of six hundred millions, when our territory shall be fully occupied. It is almost certain that an improving system of agriculture will very greatly increase these capacities, and that one person to each acre, or 640 to the mile, in the fourth grade, would not be an excessive estimate.* We have not assumed population rates beyond those actually existing. Thus England and Wales have a population of 340 to the square mile, France 183, the Austrian Empire 146, Prussia 163, the Kingdom of Italy 216, Belgium 411, Massachusetts 157.83, and Rhode Island 133.71. When it is remembered how large a portion of these states is occupied by unproductive mountains, and that our prairie soil is unequaled in fertility, our assumed rates cannot be found extravagant.

The actual movement of our population through seven decades, as shown by eight census enumerations, is as follows: 3,929,827 in 1790; 5,305,925 in 1800; 7,239,814 in 1810; 9,638,131 in 1820; 12,866,020 in 1830; 17,069,453 in 1840; 23,191,876 in 1850; 31,448,322 in 1860, or 31,747,514, including Indian tribes, etc. The ratios of increase in these successive decades are, 35.02 in 1790—

---

* A writer in the Encyclopedia Britannica goes so far as to estimate that the New World can support a population of 3,600,000,000, which would give to the United States a much larger quota than we have supposed.

1800, and successively, 36.45; 33.13; 33.49; 32.67; 35.87; 35.59; and the average rate is 34.6. This rate slightly exceeds that assumed by Malthus in his proposition that a nation, unrestricted in its supply of food, will double in twenty-five years. Taking the rate of increase per decade at 33.33, we find 42,332,374 for 1870; 56,443,165 for 1880; 75,257,553 for 1890; 100,343,404 for 1900; 133,791,205 for 1910. · Making due allowances for all probable hindrances and drawbacks, we can hardly doubt that, in fifty years from this time, there will be, or at least *ought* to be, over a hundred millions of people within the present territory of the United States. A continued application of the Malthusian rate will give 63,498,562 in 1885; 126,997,124 in 1910; 253,994,248 in 1935; 507,988,496 in 1960; 1,015,967,982 in 1985. Thus this rule, which, for 80 years past, falls short of our actual increase of population, gives us in a century and a quarter over a thousand millions. It is not too much soberly and after reasonable allowances, to expect, that, in case our Union is preserved, and our normal growth permitted, our people will number at least six hundred millions before fourteen new decades shall bring in the year 2000. True statesmanship consists not in the cunning management of political parties, or in the crafty handling of foreign relations, but in giving to the far-off future its rightful consideration in the policy of to-day. The six hundred millions who are entitled to inhabit our land in the year 2000, have as true a right to influence our present policy, as has the transient *personnel* of the passing generation. No man is fit to have a potential voice in the conduct of our national affairs, still less to bear the honored name of *statesman*, for whom the developed America of the future is not a living and consistent reality by which he habitually and conscientiously shapes his present course. Prophets foretell, but statesmen foreact.

The progress of the United States in physical prosperity has even exceeded that of its population; thus confirming the reasonableness of the anticipations now stated. The total value of **our domestic** manufactures in 1850, exclusive of amounts under $500 **per annum,** was $1,019,106,616, and in 1860, this value was nineteen hundred **millions, or** $60.61 **per** capita of our population. The increase was 86 per cent. in the decade, and 123 per cent. greater than that of **the white** population in the same time. The increase of annual **value** of our manufactured products from 1850 to 1860 considerably exceeds our present national debt. Our manufactures employ 1,100,000 **men and** 285,000 women, directly supporting about one sixth **of** our population, **and indirectly** supporting another sixth, or a third directly and indirectly. The following table, shows the values and the ratio **of increase in ten years of some** of our chief manufactured products :

	1850.	1860.	Per cent. increase.
Flour and Meal..............	$135,897,806	$223,144,369	64.2
Agricultural implements......	6,842,611	17,802,514	160.1
Pig Iron..........	13,491,898	19,487,790	44.4
Bar and **rolled Iron**..........	15,938,786	22,248,796	39.5
Steam Engines and Machinery	27,998,334	47,118,550	68.2
Iron Founding..............	26,111,517	28,546,656	42.
Coal.....................	7,173,750	19,365,765	169.9
Clothing..................	43,678,802	64,002,975	47.
Lumber...................	58,521,976	95,912,286	63.9
Cotton goods..............	65,501,687	115,137,926	75.78
Woolen goods	45,261,764	68,865,963	52.
Leather....	37,791,873	63,090,751	66.9
Boots and Shoes............	53,857,036	89,549,900	67.8

In 1850, our banking capital was $227,469,077 ; in 1860, it was $421,890,095. In 1850, the true value of real estate and personal property in the United States, was $7,135,780,228, and in 1860, it was $16,159,616,068 ; the increase being $8,925,481,011, or 126.45 per cent. In 1850 there were 113,032,614 acres of occupied farm lands improved, and 180,528,000 unimproved. In 1860, these amounts had advanced to 163,261,389 and 264,508,244, or fifty millions of acres were brought under improvement in the decade. The cash value of farms was $3,271,575,426 in 1850, and $6,650,872,507 or over double in 1860. The value of farming implements and machinery was returned in 1850 at $151,587,638, and at $248,027,496 in 1860. The value of live stock in 1850 was $544,180,516, and in 1860 it was $1,107,490,216, or it more than doubled in the decade. The tobacco crop advanced from 199,752,655 lbs. in 1850, to 429,390,771 lbs. in 1860, and cotton advanced from 2,445,793 bales to 5,198,077. The value of slaughtered animals rose from $111,703,142 to $212,871,653. Our railroad system exhibits the most remarkable increase, from 8,589 miles, costing $296,660,148 in 1850, to 30,793 miles, costing $1,151,560,829 in 1860. No candid and sagacious mind can fail to see in these typical facts of a decade, which show a physical progress so far exceeding our increase of population, the real and well assured foundation for a future national growth at least equal to the preceding estimate. It remains to be seen how far the blight of secession will frustrate our normal development.

Two great anomalies pervade and vitiate our national progress. *Race and caste* create discords where all should be harmony. *Black and white, slave and free,* are our two serious national problems, and problems which we shall be compelled to solve.*

---

* Historically, these problems stand as follows: Our total *colored* population was 757,363 in 1790; 1,001,436, in 1800; 1,377,810 in 1810; 1,771,562 in 1820; 2,328,642 in 1830; 2,873,758 in 1840; 3,638,762 in 1850, and 4,441,765 in 1860. The decadal ratios of increase are (1790—1800), 32.23; 37.58; 28.58; 31.45; 23.41; 26.62; 22.07; averaging 28.85, against 34.6 for our total, and the decadal ratio of colored increase is 0.834 or five sixths the ratio of increase of our whole population, and 0.806 or four fifths that of our

Science is not lacking in definite instruction upon the question of races. As each animal species has its own limits of habitation on the earth's surface beyond which it cannot flourish, so have the varieties of the **human race**. There are tropical races and there are temperate **races, each thriving** only in its own proper climate. The man of **the tropics not** only belongs within the tropics, but **suffers by transfer to** colder regions. Thus, in Rhode Island or Connecticut, **the** deaths of blacks and mulattoes exceed the births, and in Boston they are nearly as two to one. The man of the temperate zone deteriorates by transfer within the tropics. Climates and races are in such definite mutual adaptation, **that** it is above all needful to have the right man in the right **place.** The United States territory lies wholly in the north temperate or truly historic zone, and, **as a broad natural** fact, it belongs to the temperate races. The **Caucasian race,** under

white population. If we allow for white immigration, the ratio of **increase in** the colored population will exceed that of the whites. The total **number of** alien passengers arriving in the United States, most of whom were emigrants, was, from 1820–1830, 151,824; 1831–40, 599,125; 1841–50, 1,713,251; 1851–60, 2,598,214; 1820–60, 5,062,414. The *slave* population was **697,897** in 1790; 893,041 in 1800; 1,191,364 in 1810; 1,538,038 in 1820; **2,009,043 in** 1830; 2,487,455 in 1840; 3,204,313 in 1850; 3,953,760 **in 1860.** The ratios of increase are 27.97; 33.40; 28.79; 30.61; **23.91; 28.82;** 23.39; averaging 28.11. The *free-colored* population **was** 59,466 in 1790; 108,395 in 1800; 186,446 in 1810; 233,524 in **1820;** 319,599 in 1830; 386,303 in 1840; 434,449 in 1850; 488,005 in 1860; **and** the ratios of increase were 82.28; 72.00; 25.23; 36.87; 20.87; 12.46; 12.33, averaging 37.43, **or** nearly three eighths. The *white* population was 3,172,464 in **1790; 4,304,489** in 1800; 5,862,004 in 1810; 7,861,937 in 1820; 10,537,**378 in 1830;** 14,195,695 in 1840; 19,553,114 in 1850; 26,975,575 in 1860, and the ratios of increase were 35.68; 36.18; 34.11; 34.03; 34.72; **37.74;** 37.97, averaging 35.78. The average ratios of increase in seven decades are then: *total population*, 34.60; *white*, 35.78; *colored*, 28.85; *free colored*, 37.43; *slave*, 28.11. A careful examination of these data will **show** the tendencies of our population development.

various nationalities, has full possession of Europe, and in the westward march of empire has colonized our country. North America directly confronts Europe, and naturally derives its colonization thence. Fostered by progress in civilization, population has already become excessive in parts of Europe, and seeks its outlet in America. In the grand order of historic progress, North America belongs to the Caucasian race, the most powerful and actively colonizing branch of the human family. Regarded as a question in the natural history of man, there can be no denial of the title by which Europe has claimed and will claim the right to colonize North America. The great western movement along parallels, climate, and natural adaptation, so ordain. Europe alone sends hither voluntary colonists, if we except the Chinese emigration on the Pacific coast, which is a misdirection of a tropical race, and should not be encouraged. Caucasian civilization has an overmastering vitality and reality, which not only gives it superior power, but a higher right to expand and assert itself. The Indian title has rightly been swept away before the colonizing demands of the highest earthly civilization, and no inferior race is privileged to bar its progress over the New World.

Our country is not a natural home for the negro, and he is only here on compulsion. He belongs within the tropics, whence he came. There are immense unclaimed tropical regions, which the white man can never till. Caucasians will soon want all the temperate lands of the earth. Thus the African, of all men most tropical, can only be permanently in temperate regions by perversion and *misposition*. He would never of his own accord go beyond vertical sunshine. He never has attained, and by his own act never would attain, a high organizing civilization, without which he can have no serious need of colonization. It seems an immense sin against

4

nature that white men, stimulated by a wicked lust of gain, should have torn the sons of the equator from their tropic homes and transferred them to a land which Caucasians must, in the progress of time, claim wholly for themselves. But God educes good from human transgression, and we gratefully recognize that Divine beneficence which even converts the forced African colonization of our country into a blessing for the African. We can see that Africa, left to itself, would merely continue its poor barbaric history, without progress or colonization. By the slave system in this country, a large number of this tropical race have reached higher civilization than they otherwise could have done. They have learned so to live that their increase equals or exceeds that of our own race, under the most favoring conditions. The superior sagacity of white men, stimulated by the base profits of slave-breeding and slave-labor, has not only made the negroes fearfully prolific, but has so ordered their circumstances of daily life as greatly to promote their health and longevity: a result due in large part also to the praiseworthy humanity of their masters. The slave population, particularly in the cotton states, thus shows a truly threatening rate of increase, which well deserved serious attention from those whose domestic future was wholly involved in this portentous cloud, and whose children were in danger of drowning in an African black sea. If white men are to hold the cotton states, negro fecundity must be counteracted, or the negro race must be deported.

The main question is, shall these states be hopelessly Africanized, or shall they be reclaimed for the sole use of the white man? If we look ahead even a single century, we cannot fail to see that every acre of our domain, on which white men can live, will inevitably be required by our own race. It would be in thorough contravention of the natural order of human progress to give up half our country in perpetuity to a tropical race, so inferior in capacity and culture as to inspire no hope of their attaining a high civilization. That these negroes are held in slavery to white masters does not alter the cardinal fact, that a country perfectly adapted to occupancy by a pure white race is being perverted, contrary to nature, for negro habitation. We can never, under any shallow pretext of occupation by a few white masters, assent to the virtual annexation, forever, of half our domain to Africa. We have but to look at the relative increase of blacks and whites in the slave states, to recognize the alarming fact of utter Africanization looming in the near future. How lamentable is their fallacy, who, because the African is inferior to our race, would, under the figment of slavery, surrender to him forever more than half our territory! When there shall be ten, twenty, or a hundred blacks to one white, even though the relation of master and slave remain unaltered, can it be said that those states belong to white men? Admit that all the profits of all the labor go into the pockets of a few white men; does this even mitigate the great foundation fact of forfeiture from white to black tenure?

Towering far above the social problem of slavery or freedom for the negro, rises this momentous question of races. It is happily true that the white race is every way the strongest, and that strength must ultimately conquer. In numbers, in increase, in civilization, in adaptation, the white race has the superiority within our national domain, and the African must inevitably be eliminated. It will be a great duty of our future to remove the negro humanely to his proper tropical home. The white race, which has by violence forced Africa into the temperate zone, must transfer the negro to his natural inter-tropical American home so kindly as to make amends for past wrongs.

As we calmly contemplate this problem in the natural history of races, the impression powerfully grows upon us, that our great misplacement of Africans within the temperate zone, on lands predestined for a temperate race, has been Divinely permitted, as the condition of a progress otherwise impracticable. We cannot but connect our negro problem with the still mysterious future of the *Amazon* valley. The greatest and most fertile river basin in the world must be designed for some proportionate use. God never made this magnificent garden of tropical luxuriance without some purpose of human habitation. Africa stands over against the mouth of the great river of the equator, as if destined, in the westward march of colonization, to give its surplus population to this vast and fruitful realm, which nature forever consecrates to the children of the sun. It seems to us that the misposition of Africans in our own land, may have been permitted as a needed step in the transfer of a cultivated negro colonization to the plains of the Maranon. These plains are closed to all except African and Southern Asiatic labor. The inert African would never move on alone to this imperial destiny. Obviously his training in the Southern states will make him vastly better fitted to work out a worthy future for his race in equatorial South America. The superior intelligence of the white man being thus effectively impressed upon him, he can go to the Amazon Valley better prepared to achieve enduring progress. The true solution of the whole negro problem may, perhaps, be found in a destined **African** empire of the Amazon, to be founded by our deported negroes, previously so far civilized by their enforced and abnormal contact with our race, that they can wisely govern themselves in some congenial form of tropical organization. There is apparently no other solution for our race problem, than that which is based on a policy of graduated but energetic *deport-*

ation.   Amalgamation is abhorrent and, as a fixed policy, utterly impracticable by decent methods. The perpetuation of the existing order of castes, or a resolution into free white and free black castes, cannot be accepted as the law of our future. Nothing less than the gradual elimination of the negro element by deportation from all our lands where white men can live and labor, will meet the clearly perceptible exactions of our coming development and growth.

The South American continent is strikingly similar in structure to our own, contrasting chiefly in being tropical and sub-tropical, while ours is temperate and arctic. A like triangular continental plain, buttressed against the Andes, presents similar vast surfaces of low relief, drained by the La Plata waters as the analogue of the Mississippi, while the Amazon corresponds to the Lakes and St. Lawrence. The Brazilian coast ranges and the Appalachians, the Andes and the Rocky Mountains, the narrow Pacific slopes, the broad North and pointed South extremities, are features of structural analogy. Fortunately, the vast plain of the Amazon, out-measuring one and a half Mississippi Valleys, is liberally watered by a rain-fall exceeding even that of our Gulf states, while the climate is greatly mitigated by the trade-winds. The abounding forests, which fringe the **great river and** its tributaries, proves that exhaustless fertility of soil awaits development. The negro, naturally proof against heat and miasms, is even better fitted than the Southern Asiatic to battle with these primeval groves. **Possibly** the effete civilization of China or Japan, is here destined to flower forth in some new and vital manifestation, but the African seems providentially on the colonizing road toward the equatorial empire of the future. Already had Brazil three millions of slaves, and half a million of free negroes, out of a population estimated at five millions in 1848. It can only be through a scientific and truly statesmanlike grasp of the vast possibilities for the future, now dormant in the West Indies and South America, but especially in Brazil, that publicists will be able correctly to solve the great problem concerning the proper adjustment of the now ill-understood relations of habitation and intercourse between the tropical and temperate races. A mere fragment of this adjustment is now intrusted to our charge, but the right treatment of our negro controversy can only result from a clear view of the whole earth problem of races. Statesmanship which does not proceed on this broad and truly scientific basis, can only result in disaster, when it attempts to direct and control the territorial distribution of races. This is the fatal error of those who would push the negro, whether as slave or freeman, away from the tropics into regions consecrated to white labor.

[While waiting the providential restoration of the Americanized Africans to their appropriate tropical home, it is, meantime, a matter of serious regret, and of permanent detriment to the Caucasian race, that negro agriculture, whether as slave or free, is wasting the native fertility of the Southern soil. During the vast primeval ages, a process has been slowly operating by which the falling leaves have borne down, from the air into the soil, their carbonized and nitrogenized products. The accumulated fertility of ages has thus been stored in anticipation of the coming agricultural period. The thriftless system of exhausting lands, which seems inseparable from the rude and unintelligent labor of the negro, whether slave or free, and the successive occupancy of new plantations as old ones are worn out, can only end in the ultimate, general impoverishment of the States where the system prevails. A nation's true material wealth must ever consist chiefly in the fertile capacity of its lands; in the carbonaceous and nitrogenized ingredients of its soil. These once exhausted, desolation and poverty must prevail.

The worn-out lands of Virginia, and the desolate circuit of abandoned plantations, which for fifty miles environs Havana, are monumental protests against such frauds on the soil. There will, moreover, be peculiar difficulty in winning back fertility to Southern soils by the agricultural skill of free white labor. The lack of luxuriant and nutritious grasses in the Southern states, is not only a source of present privations, but it takes from the farmer his chief means of making good the waste of the planter. Thus, the temporary sway of slave or negro labor, threatens to make an irretrievable desert of the lands, from which it is now recklessly exhausting that fertility, which the forest ages have been storing up. When the African shall reach the Valley of the Amazon, he will find a soil, practically inexhaustible, but his enforced residence in our Southern temperate lands seems to be inwrought with the promise of a retributive calamity, a coming curse of barrenness, from which there will be no rescue, save in the weary toil of unborn generations of free white laborers. The urgent motive thus supplied to work out without needless delay, the providential policy of friendly deportation, is one whose force will be most felt by the most humane and philosophical minds.]*

Every worthy idea of human nature and the human lot, whether derived from historic, social or moral considerations, exalts freedom and deprecates slavery. It was reserved for our generation to hear the gospel of slavery zealously proclaimed, and, like a new Islamism, propagated by the sword. We have seen eleven states formally abjuring the dearly-bought faiths of freedom, and extolling slavery as a blessing in itself. Holding that the negro belongs to an inferior race

* [ ] January, 1863.

they would yet force him into regions congenial for white labor. The slave-holding leaders would sustain and glorify their peculiar institution as the Ephesians did Diana; while "the poor whites" of the South, fearing that negro freedom would involve an equality fatal to their own shabby gentility, and utterly ignorant of the true dignity of labor, fight in illogical concert, little realizing that they are striving to Africanize their own states, to the ultimate exclusion of their own offspring. Whatever be the immediate issue of the contest now pending, its future progress toward the triumph of freedom, and Caucasianism is naturally assured. Freedom is stronger than slavery, the Caucasian is stronger than the African, and, historically, the North has been "the hive of nations," which have swarmed in conquering progress southward. *Free, white, Northern* strength must ultimately exclude *slave, black, Southern* domination from the area now in controversy, either by equitable, pacific progress, or by warlike violence. Should we now enact any weak concessions to Southern pro-slavery fanaticism, our posterity will disown our attorneyship, and will re-enact that law of Nature, which gives the seceded states to European, and the Empire of the Amazon to African emigration. The sacred *democracy* which founds the social organism on man's simple humanity, which recognizes human nature as Divine in origin, character, and destiny, which honors labor and exalts the laborer, which hopefully strives to make the future ever better than the past in a growing progress, which, amid all discouragements, and proofs of man's imperfection, ever lovingly holds fast to the noblest ideal of aspiring, struggling, enduring, triumphant manhood; this universal and unpartisan democracy, which through ages of travail has painfully and solemnly labored into life, now lives, and will forever live, strong in the right, and upborne in all conflicts with ancient wrong and privilege, by the vital energy which God has implanted in man's nature. Our fidelity to this heritage of regulated and organized freedom, will guide and guard our national progress, and, as years, decades, and centuries roll on, will establish our nationality ever more firmly on UNION FOUNDATIONS.

POSTSCRIPT.

The progress of public events since the preceding pages were written, has been conformed to the principles therein defined. Human passions have indeed, during the entire progress of the pending controversy, been too actively engaged to permit the free and full working of those great natural agencies to which the ultimate issue of the contest is rightfully committed. It is human passion which has fired our noble temple of Union, founded in an heroic age and adorned by the living virtues of three generations. Nothing but hot anger or frenzied delusion, could have made parricides of men who are our kindred, who were nurtured under the tutelage of the Constitution, who shared all our proud historic memories, and who, by all the titles of common lineage, language, culture, growth and hopes, were with us in one nation and under one banner. Vinegar is sugar fermented: the bitterest feuds, the most relentless hates, are also the tenderest and dearest affections transformed. But as nature produces no vinegar except by changing sweet to sour, so human hearts are not born imbued with hate, and the bad access of vengeful feeling which marks the bitter controversy of to-day, must die out if it be not studiously nurtured in the rising generations. The unity of race and language, which is an unchangeable fact, must assert itself in the future as in the past. The negro and the social order based on his inferiority, forming as they do, the sole divellent forces, which strive to rend asunder that which God has joined together, must not be permitted to breed eternal discord in our land. The time must come when reason will be heard, and then the African, who is the fruitful, but innocent source of all our woes, will go hence where he belongs. With him will go all those mad ambitions of oligarchy which, building caste on color, now war on the very citadel of democratic freedom. God grant, too, that with the negro may depart that fanatical benevolence, so malevolent in its manifestations, whose bitter fruitage we taste and execrate. God has His own ways of working, and however slow these methods may seem, it is not wise for man to try whipping up. It is well to realize that the Creator of the world and of man still lives, and is responsible for the general progress of events. "Learn to labor and to wait," is a mandate of Divine order for nations as for men. It will be a blessed day when peace shall crown reason, when patient, earnest work shall soften hearts now hard with hate, and when fraternal Union under the Constitution, shall nurture into new and enduring life, a loyalty, heart-felt and universal, toward that great nation and national work which Supreme Wisdom has here predestined.

Ere this can be we must purge away a great national sin. A demoralized political system which converts public trusts into partisan spoils, has killed true statesmanship, and made the growth of statesmen nearly impossible. Hence the foundation elements, the eternal principles, have not received that recognition which was their right.

The lack of leadership which is now felt as our sorest national affliction, is but the natural retribution on our people for the political dereliction, which has given over the beneficent and holy functions of government to harpies, while the great and good have been left unsought and undeveloped in the genial shades of private life. To ask great statesmen or great leaders under this monstrous system, is to ask effects without causes. Some great affliction was sure to result from the "spoils" system, and had not secession grown out of it, something else as bad was in duty bound to punish us. There can be no hope for us, except in a renewal of political integrity, which will enable us again to restore the government to its pristine virtue. A counter-revolution which shall reinstate the public offices in their old glory, as honorable trusts, confided to the most honest and capable, and which shall end their degradation to the base uses of party, will revive all our dear old hopes, now bowed in the sorrow of disgrace. No opulence of natural bounty can give true prosperity to a people so demoralized as patiently to endure *systematic official simony*. God be thanked that this war has shown us how noble, and patient, and hopeful our people are, and that this execrable perversion of official tenures is thus proven to be no real exponent of our national morality. Self-government on a devil-worshiping basis, is simply hell's unendurable horror; but a nation governing itself in sincere natural piety, and in profound regard for Heaven-born right, cannot fail to triumph over all afflictions, and emerge triumphant from all trials. God has so framed human and material nature as to ensure the ultimate exaltation of a righteous nation. Amid the sorrows of the present, it is consoling to recognize God's government, which chastens to heal, which works on in solemn silence through all the varying phases of our contest, and which will uphold American unity, if our own unworthiness shall not unfit us to realize His thoughts and designs, as embodied in the physical features of our national domain.

The preceding discussion legitimately leads us to the conclusion that one of three events must close the contest now joined:

1st. The restoration of the Constitutional Union, as a result of the war in progress.

2d. Temporary disunion, until the Confederacy, based on slavery as its chief corner-stone, shall recognize its impending doom in the overwhelming growth of free white labor, and shall seek the restoration of the Union by friendly means, and on a truly democratic basis.

3d. Temporary disunion, until the blinded and defiant Confederacy, by holding the boundary line drawn tight against free white labor, and the democratic spirit of progress, shall again evoke the desolating scourge of war, and thus meet its final fate.

In each of these contingencies, the perpetuation of the Union should only be regarded as a question of time and growth. Any failure now to effect its restoration will simply remit the completion of the contest to a future generation. The exasperations and arrogances hitherto so conspicuously displayed by the Southern leaders, afford but slender ground for hope that the second solution would result from a present relinquishment of our warlike strife, and the evolution of some unnatural boundary. Our main question of to-day seems to be between the completion of the Union contest *now* and its resumption from the beginning in a still greater future war, which can hardly be postponed through fifty years. When we consider the woes unutterable which our failure would entail on our posterity, the sad obstruction to all progress in good culture and humane development, the bitter anguish of hostile feeling thus made enduring, the bereavements and heart-aches of to-day, renewed on a scale greatly enlarged; when, with serious and sad hearts, we confront the future, which must thus be born from our actions in this crucial year, we can only say, God help us bravely to do what is right and wise !

It is ever the heroic endurance of the last weeks of war which shapes the conditions of peace. It is our duty to work out now, if possible, a peace which shall endure. Such good fruit can only grow from the rich soil of old fraternity and of new purposes of right, justice, moderation, and good will. Restored Union means restored citizenship and renewed brotherhood. Our armed assertion of this great Nation's Divinely ordered unity, must keep companionship with a humane spirit of overmastering fraternity. There are other weapons than firearms with which to reclaim the truant and erring. The forgiving heart, the home welcome, the tender oblivion of follies and wrongs, the kindly nurture of returning affection and the generous justice in which magnanimous natures delight; these must do a work which is beyond the chemistry of gunpowder, ere a living and vital Union can again send its glad pulses through the healthful body of our renewed nation. This we owe, not to soothe Confederate pride, but as a natural fruit of our own earnest loyalty to the great obligations of American Nationality.

Whatever may be the destined "issue out of all our afflictions," the importance of rescuing our government from its perversions and reinvesting it with the majesty of pure purpose, exalted ideas, high capacity, secured stability, and faithful execution, remains paramount.

NEW HAVEN, CONN.,
    January 20, 1863.

www.ingramcontent.com/pod-product-compliance
Lightning Source LLC
Chambersburg PA
CBHW030854260626
47169CB00008B/2539